Having a Hearing Test

Vic Parker

www.raintreepublishers.co.uk
Visit our website to find out
more information about
Raintree books.

To order:
☎ Phone 0845 6044371
🖷 Fax +44 (0) 1865 312263
🖳 Email myorders@raintreepublishers.co.uk

Customers from outside the UK please telephone +44 1865 312262

Raintree is an imprint of Capstone Global Library
Limited, a company incorporated in England and Wales
having its registered office at 7 Pilgrim Street, London,
EC4V 6LB – Registered company number: 6695582

Edited by Dan Nunn, Rebecca Rissman, and Sian Smith
Designed by Joanna Hinton-Malivoire
Picture research by Elizabeth Alexander
Originated by Capstone Global Library Ltd
Printed and bound in China by Leo Paper
Products Ltd

ISBN 978 1 406 22048 3 (hardback)
15 14 13 12 11
10 9 8 7 6 5 4 3 2 1

British Library Cataloguing in Publication Data
Parker, Victoria.
   Having a hearing test. – (Growing up)
   1. Audiometry–Pictorial works–Juvenile literature.
   2. Hearing clinics–Pictorial works–Juvenile literature.
   I. Title II. Series

617.8'9-dc22

Acknowledgements
We would like to thank the following for permission to
reproduce photographs: Alamy pp. 9 (© NewStock),
14 (© Bubbles Photolibrary), 21, 23 glossary hearing
aid (© kavring); © Capstone Publishers p. 17 (Karon
Dubke); Corbis pp. 6 (© Ariel Skelley/Blend Images), 7
(© Corbis), 18 (© Patrick Lane/Somos Images); Getty
Images pp. 20, 23 glossary operation (David Leahy/
Cultura); iStockphoto p. 15 (© Carmen Martínez Banús);
Photolibrary pp. 10, 23 glossary expert (Javier Larrea/
age footstock), 11 (David Leahy/Cultura), 12 (BL BL/BSIP
Medical), 16, 19 (Image Source); Shutterstock pp. 4 (©
Monkey Business Images), 5 (© Sean Prior), 8 (© AVAVA),
13 (© Ronald Sumners).

Front cover photograph of a boy having a hearing test
reproduced with permission of Getty (Ross Whitaker/
The Image Bank). Back cover photographs of an ear
reproduced with permission of Shutterstock (© Monkey
Business Images), and a school nurse reproduced with
permission of Shutterstock (© AVAVA).

We would like to thank Jane Jones for her invaluable
help in the preparation of this book.

Contents

Some words are shown in bold, **like this**.
You can find them in the glossary on page 23.

What is a hearing test?

ear

You hear sound through your ears.

You can see part of your ear outside your head, but there are other parts inside your head too.

A hearing test checks that all the parts of your ears are working properly.

It will show if you can hear all sorts of low and high sounds.

When might I have a hearing test?

You may have had a hearing test when you were a baby.

You may have another hearing test when you start school.

Sometimes your teacher, parent, or doctor might think you have a problem with your hearing.

You may have a hearing test then, too.

Where will it happen?

Your hearing test may take place at school.

You may have to go to the school nurse's room or the office for the test.

You might go to see your doctor for a hearing test.

Or you might go for your test at a hospital.

Who will I meet?

If you have a hearing test at school, someone will come in to show you what to do.

They will be an **expert** who knows about ears and hearing.

A hearing test might be done by your family doctor or nurse.

If you have a hearing test in a hospital, you may meet a special kind of doctor.

What type of equipment will I see?

headphones

You may see a machine which makes different sorts of sounds.

You listen to the sounds through headphones.

The person doing your hearing test may have a small tool with an end that fits inside your ear.

They look through this to see into your ear.

What will I have to do?

The doctor or nurse will help you put on the headphones.

They will ask you to do particular things whenever you hear certain sounds.

When they look into your ears, they will ask you to sit very still.

They are checking that the inside of your ear is the right shape and is not blocked.

Will the hearing test hurt?

It is natural to feel a little nervous about your hearing test.

However, nothing will hurt you.

It can be strange to wear headphones or let somebody look into your ears.

But everything the doctor or nurse does is to help you.

What happens if there is a problem?

Sometimes a hearing test can show that you have a problem with your ears.

You may need to have further tests to work out exactly what this is.

A doctor might give you medicine for some ear problems.

This can make your ears better again.

What other help might people get?

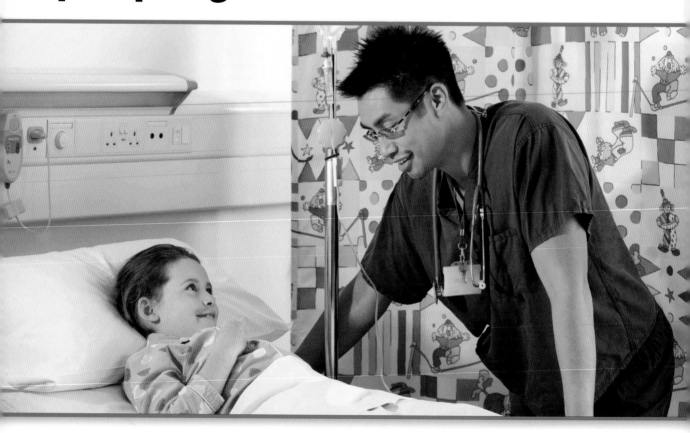

Some people might need an **operation** to solve a hearing problem.

Before the operation, they are given medicine so they do not feel anything.

hearing aid

Some people are given a **hearing aid**.

People wear hearing aids in their ears to help them to hear better.

Tips to keep your ears healthy

Do:

✓ remember to put sunblock on your ears when you are out in the sun

✓ wear a hat to keep your ears warm when it is cold

✓ remember to dry your ears well after you have been swimming.

Don't:

✗ listen to very loud music

✗ stick things into your ears.

Picture glossary

 **expert** someone who knows a lot about something and has special skills in that area

 **hearing aid** tiny machine that fits in your ear, which helps you to hear things better

 **operation** in an operation, a doctor gives you medicine to put you to sleep while they try to make you better

Find out more

Books

Healthy Eyes and Ears (Look After Yourself), Angela Royston (Heinemann Library, 2006)

Hearing (The Senses), Mandy Suhr (Wayland 2007)

Now Hear This!: The Secrets of Ears and Hearing (Gross and Goofy Body), Melissa Stewart and Janet Hamlin (Benchmark Books, 2009)

Websites

Learn more about hearing and other parts of your body at:
kidshealth.org/kid/

Discover more about your amazing ears at:
www.childrenfirst.nhs.uk

Index